To The Flowers That Bloomed

J.J. Paulson

To The Flowers That Bloomed
Paperback

ISBN: 979-8-218-90002-1

Published & Printed in The United States of America

Website: www.JJPaulson.com

Instagram: @J.J.Paulson

Email: Sales@jjpaulson.com

Dedications:

To my sons: "May you bloom brightly. With love &
kindness for yourselves, and all inhabitants of this beautiful
world."

To all the love that has come and gone, and for all those still
here. I am grateful and I thank you. For it is you who have
watered my soul and aided my growth. And I hope this, in
some way, can return that favor.

Dear Reader:

I hope this book serves as a seed of inspiration; in whatever journey you are in life. Continue to nurture that seed with love, so that you may face life with goodness in your heart and allow those roots to spread and sprout across the world.

My Writing Inspiration:

It is a true joy to finally share the passion of vulnerability to pen. I've been writing songs and poems in secrecy for a long time, as an outward expression of things I can't relay with the spoken word. This is the first introduction of my work in a public manner.

I find myself drawn to the beauty and darkness of this world. The cohesion and juxtaposition of those two elements. Like black and white photographs or major and minor keys; they create a yin & yang in my mind.

I often want to pay homage to my muses.
I am inspired by all manners of art forms. When I hear music, I visualize short films in my mind. How the music matches the scenery of nature, life in motion, a drive, or just my everyday being. What I see and hear blending together and played back to me. Sometimes a line from a song, a book, a poem, or even a movie/show can inspire me to write around that idea. I might see a character or a moment and build a story. My imagination can take art and the natural scenery of this world and paint pictures, which I try to incapsulate in the written word. Immortalizing the moments I find beautiful.

4

What inspired "To The Flowers That Bloomed":

This book is conceptual. A theme I thought of in the midst of earnest introspection for me, and a sort of apology to all of those I may have wronged in my life. As well as an apology to myself. It is self critical but allows room for growth and healing. I hope you enjoy reading it as much as I have enjoyed writing it. I genuinely love it and hope it becomes a small staple in your book collection.

Of all the flowers to bloom

In a world of beauty and gloom

This is my proof –

That I picked you

Dawn

Dusk

Darkness

To The Flowers That Bloomed

Dawn

Dawn

It is in the still of the morning

The twilight of dawn

Where the Sun begins its ascent

Into a golden hour

Painting a canvas full of blood orange hues

When the Earth is still silent and sound asleep

And there is nothing

But the quiet contemplation

Of You and Your thoughts

The first inhalation

A breath of fresh air to renew the spirit

Before the caffeinated veins

Begin their seizures to seize the new day

I feel a moment of peace

Before the world awakens

The One with the Sun

It's somewhere in a dream
Or some future memory
Like a warm home movie on celluloid film
With light breaking through the trees
Bending and fracturing through the window

I see her lit

The glowing flares flicker behind
Haloed by the sun surrounding her silhouette
Chromatic aberrations of colors fringing;
the spectrum of light refracting through its prism
A vignette written in the lens of my eyes

Her skin, porcelain
Kissed with a golden flawless shine

That's how I know she's the One
She's the one with the Sun

Sunflower

It is there
Everyday
My only sunshine
When I walk out into the yard
On the building across from mine
The only beautiful thing I see
In this cage
Bright as the Summer days it blossoms in
It's all I look forward to seeing
And just like that
I am free
And it is gone
A momentary memory
In my mind
That sunflower
Still there
I sat and waited for its return
While it teased me of a future never to come
Now I sit and wait for my ride home
As the gate closes behind
The yellow iris reflects in my eyes
One last time

Morning Glory

In the germination of Saturday mornings
As day breaks
And the light peaks in
We are skin to skin
The heat of our bodies
Beneath the cold sheets
We play like cats
That purring pussy
Meowing at me
But 9 lives just isn't enough
For a lifetime like this
Her breath fills my lungs
As if it were my last
Forever isn't enough
To be tangled together
In the scent of Morning Glory
Oh! What glorious mornings!

The Alchemy of Coffee

On the farm
Sprouts the cherry
Shaped by soil it did not choose
Absorbing its role without protest
Believing itself complete
Unaware of its sweet potential
Beneath lies a deeper truth–
That its essence is hidden within the seed

In its first loss,
Comes separation
Detaching from what sustained it
Its flesh stripped away
And exposed is the seed within
Left bare in open air
Naked and uncertain
Humble and unfinished
Alive yet dormant
Green and waiting
It rests in a long patience
But closer than ever to its essence

Into the fire
It's tossed
The catalyst of irreversible change
Alchemy turning green into roasted gold

As the roast progresses
Pressure builds, the seed swells
The bean cracks
First in protest, then in surrender
What is not needed burns away
What remains darkens & deepens
Sugars turn to shadow & sweetness
Pain becomes aroma
In the flame, essence awakens
Revealing what was always there
A complexity it's never known

Finally, broken down again
Not by fire, but by intention
Made permeable for the final transmutation
Meeting the ancient solvent
In the hot water it bathes
Blooming then moving
Through the membranes of dimensions
All beans becoming one
Brewing just long enough
To become everything they were meant to be
Balanced & complex
Awakened within
And now a shared communion
Warming the body
A cup of remembrance
Awakening the minds & souls of others

Apple Blossom

In early Spring
On the Equinox
Pink-white petals burst open
Sudden & Luminous
On bare branches
After a long winter
They don't ask how long they'll last
They bloom anyway
Soft, hopeful, and a little bit reckless
Trusting the sun, the breeze, the moment
Some carried off by wind or rain
Some fall quietly to the ground
And even when the petals are gone
Something remains–
A sweetness in the air
A promise tucked deep in the branch
Proof that once, in a brief Michigan Spring,
It was brave enough to bloom
Just for the joy of blooming

Hungover

I feel my blood buzzing with booze
Shifting, scratching, moving
Tingling the fingertips
As I lay still – lifeless
There is an acute awareness
Of the pulse pushing and pumping life
Through my veins
To be so relaxed –
Limp, numb, weightless
Beneath the dead weight
Of a breathing corpse
It's almost euphoric
If I didn't feel like shit

Flowers in Her Hair

She was birth of the Earth
Resembling the Mother in the flesh
The scent of her hair in the air
Blowing with the breeze
Spinning barefoot
Tilting my world off axis
A Queen of the wild
With her flower crown
She set my heart free

Delightful Delirium

Oh, delightful delirium
I shake in your wake
Stirring in my grave
Oh, delightful delirium
Your crooked Smile
And manic eyes
Scattered in tattered taste
Oh, delightful delirium
You dance in a hypnotic trance of disillusion
Free in the wild of dreaming
Dreams of despair
In destiny's destruction
Oh, delightful delirium
Dressed to death in dichotomy
Designed by disturbing desire
In the minds of matter
Oh, delightful delirium
You highlight Human hypocrisy
The dreadful dreary deeds
Of the dire in need
Desperate for a desolate touch
Wasted in a material race
Oh, delightful delirium
I shake in your wake
I'm intrigued by the break
Color me curious
You're delightfully delirious!

Princess

She waits

Curled in a lonely silence

She waits

By the door all day

She waits

Until my return

She waits

My approach growing near

Catching my scent

She waits

Ready to play

Overjoyed at the sight of me

Head-to-head

Staring deeply

With all sincerity

The love from my dog

Is the closest thing I've felt

To Love

In it's purity

Dandelion

Such a curious boy
Bright eyed and full of joy
He watched everything I did
I picked a dandelion while walking
He loves blowing the seeds off
And I too–
Whispering wishes into the wind

Iris

At first glance

A tender beauty

Beneath the layers

Of its hidden architecture

Is a quiet strength

Bold and unashamed

The standards and falls

Of its hilt-like petals

Stands tall

A raised sword

A rainbow

Pretty in pink

Vibrant in a violent shade of violet

The blue of its hue is true

A starlet in scarlet

A goddess of the garden

Our Secret Tongue

In the space between atoms

And the silence between breaths

Tightened lungs

Expand and release

In our secret tongues

On a shared wavelength

That frequency

...is where you'll find me

The Masquerade *

Come one, come all!
Everyone's welcomed
At The Masquerade Ball

From The Devils legion of demons
To Gods army of Angels
The corrupt & crooked capitalists
Even the plighted minimum wagers

Wallflowers need not fear
There are no faces here
We all wear masks
Through screens of the masses
Memorizing lines
Like actors and actresses

Perhaps it's a cliché
But as Shakespeare would say
All the world's a stage
We're rehearsing roles for the parts we play

Charading charlatans of the bourgeoisie
Dressed in antique pageantry
Thespians smile, parading their veneers
The dancing marionettes of puppeteers

What a night for the great pretenders
Selling their soul in a social surrender
Sinners and saints are one in the same
Living their lives in The Masquerade

Lilac

The first of many to come

We were blooming in youthful innocence

...Or ignorance

In hindsight, one can never be sure

They say you'll never forget

First love

Young love

How this Lilac

Took shape

And grew

Upward

As if to never end

But it did

As so many do

And I stood there

Alone

In the pouring rain

Watching taillights drive away

Daisy

She walked in

Looking like she was still boozing

In prohibition and pearls

Black hat and a black jacket with fur

A silver screen starlet from 1933

Her name would be

Something like Olivia, Charlotte, Ruby, or Daisy

So charming and quaint

Beautifully beguiling

Dangerously Dazzling

A poisonous kiss

Gin-soaked lips

So much life left to live

Out at the speakeasy

Playing freely

So many Daisies would come and go

I'm their one-night man

A steppingstone

Setting sails to society's plan

Before life takes course

Before the bright future fades

Into shadows of the past

Running hand in hand

With her sailor boy

Still hand in hand

Now his wife

As they walked in

Gin-soaked lips

So much life already lived

And still so much left within

So many Daisies came and went

Living lives well spent

Laleaua Mea Mică

A symbol of a new life
Blooming, blossoming, and bright
My little tulip
She Springs into Summer
Before winter has even begun
No patience this one
My Little Tulip
Seasons change
April showers
Bringing Mayflowers
As I say goodbye to the former me
Washed in the waters
Warm welcoming waves
Reawakened to a renewed life
Revitalized in the rebirth
Saying hello to a world
With My Little Tulip

The Blue Orchid

Strange how it's not even real

Of course...
Maybe That explains it

Mums

Resilient
Through Shifting seasons
Temperatures fall
Empty nests, leaves, and all
Darkening skies Plume
Like an atomic bomb
The aftershocks boom
Stirring in their hearts
And still they bring
Color to greying landscapes
All the sacrifices made
Queen of change
Queen of Autumn
For ungrateful seeds grown within
It's hard to comprehend
How magical it is...
The miracle of Mums

Dusk

Dusk

As the twilight of dusk creeps
With the fading blue hour
Shifting into a violet affair
The chem trails draw lines
Mapping the endeavors of lives
Embarked across the evening sky
The hum of the current coursing
Through the nerves of the city
Begin to wind down
The race of the day begins to steady
The sunset setting a serene scenery
The last exhales of the rush breathe relief
I feel the calm of the Earth
As it slowly slips into a sedated slumber
And I along with it...

Angel of the Night

As the stars dance around the iris of her eyes
And the moonlight brushes across her face
She illuminates the darkness with such grace
An Angel of the Night

In That Room with Lily (Our Eden)

A touch traces the tracks in my back
Pouring magic down my spine
The breath trembles
As we shared vessels
Push. Pull. Release
Shivers run down the legs
I can feel the rapid pulse
Of Our heartbeats
Synchronizing in rhythm
Tighten. Squeeze. Release
Unearthing the last of our innocence
Blooming petals opening
Finding God in that garden
This forbidden fruit
In that room
On that night
Nirvana

Paradox*

I'm surrounded by your vacancy

Overfilled with emptiness

Completely incomplete

The inertia, overly kinetic

Our ephemeral love lasting an eternity

Wallflowers & Ivy

The climbing vines

Cascading up

And fading into the wallpaper

The creature cowering in the corner

Void of social charms

Finding its secret hiding spot

The silent spectator

Observing habits

The rituals and gossip of peers

Desperate to be a part of

But camouflages in fear

Somehow still a nose above

How beautiful the ivy grows

Up the walls of a castle

So easily dismissed as

Weeds needing to be dismantled

The Rose

Born of harsh foreign soil
And riddled with thorns
It pricked me with every touch
Riddled with thorns
It bled me dry
The flower of love and romance
Or so we've been sold.
The symbol the neighbor is convinced of
What we must all strive for

I, in naive haste, picked it
This Rose
Uncertain if I'd ever find another
Just as quickly, I let it wilt
Left to rot and wither...alone
In my ignorance, fear, and doubt
I stood still, watched the still life in guilt
As it struggled to survive the drought
I saw the leaves fall frayed and torn

I could've done more
The bare minimum to say the least
Trim the stems
Prune the leaves
Keep it hydrated
Allow it some sun & air to breathe

To be fair

It deserved better care

For it did bear
The Seeds that I'd love forever
This Rose, my greatest failure
A symbol of love
Desecrated by my sinful selfishness
Upon my coffin, a single rose
Riddled with thorns
A symbol of my sorrow

To Feel Nothing and Everything, All At Once

What a strange feeling...

...Nothing...

Such a paradox

To feel the weight of Nothingness

To be spilling over with Emptiness

The remains of me

Is all that's left

I bet if they carved me open

There'd be no liver or lungs

No heart

No organs

Just flesh and bone

Shading the Shadow within

The Mortician

Breaking my chest cavity

Like crab legs

Would see

I'm just a shell of a man

A hollowed husk

Seldom do I ever feel anything truly

Or maybe I feel it all too much

The pain ever so present and persistent

It's become status quo

Find a pulse

I just want to see some vital signs

Nerves numb to being alive

In joy

In death
In love
Any emotional spectrum
Is dissolved to drained veins
Of a body once full
Now reduced to halves
Maybe quarters
Of feeling anything in totality
Something missing in all of it
Of what? I'm not sure...
But there are moments!
Where I am made whole again
Life flows through still veins
My blue lips become pink
A blush of love fills my cheeks
In those moments I can live and die full

Spirits of Bottles Past

Phantoms of the past

And spirits on the shelf

Let all the ghosts out the bottle

I'll dance with the shadows on the wall

Lunar Ruins*

Lying in lunar ruins

The gravity pulls me in

Caught in your orbit

My world revolves around you

I'm your satellite, your moon

Lost in the event horizon

Forever circling the light of your sun

You set my world into motion

The Blue Orchid (Expanded)

Strange how it's not even real

Merely a mirage

A fabricated fantasy

A dye cast

To conjure an illusion

Of something so exotic, beautiful, and true

Exaggerated expectations

Juxtaposing the Ether of Reality

And my ego, so achingly desperate,

To grasp onto the synthetic

And forgetting the flourishing beauties right in front
of me.

Of course...

Maybe That explains it

Bed of Roses

The petals lie scattered about
Like the pieces of her shattered heart
The now null and void words of the vow
Are ripped from the written pages and torn apart
The rotting roots and wilting vines
Like demure decaying limbs
Stretched across time
Turned to dust and left to whirl with the wind
Is there any hope for seeds now budding?
Will the growing sprouts thrive through each
season's cutting?
So many questions this new future poses
As we leave behind a bed of dead roses

Mayflower

Grown in stressed soil
Many others may not have survived
But to our surprise
He thrived
Though a little more–
Vulnerable
Slightly sensitive–
To disturbances
Growing slower than the Dandelion
He has a resilience
And a smile
That lasts a lifetime

How Fitting

She smelt of cigarettes

And I thought "how appropriate…"

As we smiled with regret

Lotus

It seemed something cosmic
A universal sign
She came in like a comet
With her icy trail
Burning bright
And burning out
Just as fast
As she entered my atmosphere
Something so powerful
But fleeting
The flower of life
The flower of my life

Wild Violet

Somewhere in the Adirondacks

Listening to black capped chickadees

Laying down

Looking up

Searching for the belt of Orion

As a howling wind comes sweeping in

Swirling that haunting echo

Of her voice

Quietly saying

Meet me in the stars, I'll be waiting

To the Flowers That Bloomed

I am no florist
I claim no expertise in the art of horticulture
I have never tended a garden
Nor do I have any knowledge beyond that of a novice
For a flower to thrive
I have but the most rudimentary and basic of
understandings
So, this is my apology for any damage you may have
derived
To your roots, from my neglect and ignorant
handling

You see
I am more...

The Pollinator

Leaving traces of myself upon the open petals that
welcomed me
A fleeting fertilizer
The fields of Lavender, intoxicating my senses
Blooming Roses of romance
Lilacs of love and Orchid obsessions
Shining Sunflowers and delicate Daisies
Drawing me in with its pheromonal scents
Is it a chemical instinct?
From their alluring aromatic attraction

to the curious captivating colors
So many varieties I've come to know
Come to love and nurture
Every one of them different needs to grow
But forever the fleeting fertilizer
Never allowing any to fully flourish

An artfully arranged, beautiful bouquet
Not lost, but locked away
Spreading roots
Behind my eyes
Growing in the guarded garden of my mind
Like petals in a tomb

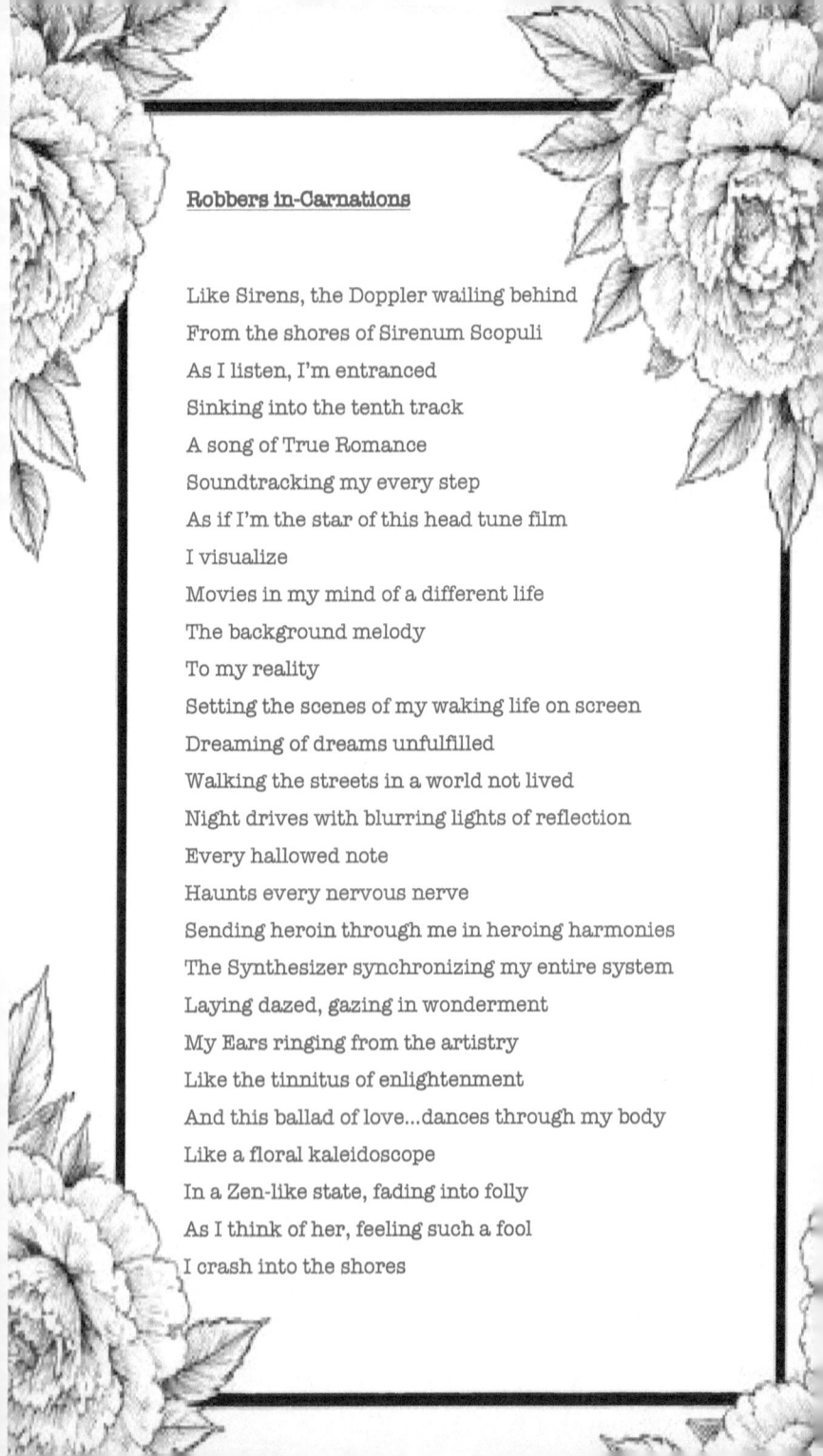

Robbers in-Carnations

Like Sirens, the Doppler wailing behind
From the shores of Sirenum Scopuli
As I listen, I'm entranced
Sinking into the tenth track
A song of True Romance
Soundtracking my every step
As if I'm the star of this head tune film
I visualize
Movies in my mind of a different life
The background melody
To my reality
Setting the scenes of my waking life on screen
Dreaming of dreams unfulfilled
Walking the streets in a world not lived
Night drives with blurring lights of reflection
Every hallowed note
Haunts every nervous nerve
Sending heroin through me in heroing harmonies
The Synthesizer synchronizing my entire system
Laying dazed, gazing in wonderment
My Ears ringing from the artistry
Like the tinnitus of enlightenment
And this ballad of love...dances through my body
Like a floral kaleidoscope
In a Zen-like state, fading into folly
As I think of her, feeling such a fool
I crash into the shores

Fading back in
He sings that closing line
As if from the top of a mountain
Screaming to the World...

She says "**Babe, you look so cool!**"

The Poet's Garden

Sifting through the detritus of our minds
Crawling grapevines wrap around bone
And through the eyes
Dropping tears of red wine
To hydrate the garden of our soul
Full of fermented fruits
Wheat and barley
Distilled in the ink in our blood
Spilling out on to the pages
Like the ancient whiskeys
Trailed on the tongue
Hedges shaped like a shifting labyrinth
Mimicking Mazes of the brain
A paradox of thought
Ranging the spectrums
From hopeful nihilists
To the burdened optimist
Seeds of doubt
Cultivated along
A starry night stroke of colors
Vast and wide
That gently bristles the mind
Archaic but aged with nuance
A harmony of chaos
...how poetic

Cherry Blossom *(A Haiku)*

A zephyr blows through

Her pretty pink petals swirl

Painting the city

The Gospel of J.J.

Falling prey to prayer
On desperate knees
Begging to be seen
In times of need
Looking to the sky
Or to pillars of worship
Paying fines
To dirty hands in money bags
Rich robes syphon poor pockets
Lost zealots create false prophets
Hearing what they need in the speech
The oppressive hypocrites
And performative devotees
Casting righteous judgment
As if they themselves are sin-free
Waging Holy Wars in the name of peace

In search of miracles,

How we pray in times of need
And forget how grateful it is to breathe!
The plight of the pious
And holier than thous
when in need,
We
Selfishly stand on a soapbox
Leaving no room for the soul to speak

We seek

and speak

and speak

But do we ever listen?

We plead for a sign

Asking for answers

Desperate for intervention from the divine

I beseech you

Hold your tongue

Quiet your mind

Still your heart

And listen!

Sit in the silence that is given

Close your eyes

And listen!

For in the depths of darkness

You will see all

And in the patience of the slow steady silence

You will hear everything

Balancing Act*

It's alarming

How you're disarming

All of my defenses

I'm straddling the fence

Between

Falling and catching myself

The Cards We Were Dealt *

We were short suited

Cutting Hearts with a Spade

Running up Clubs

& digging up Diamonds for the pain

Magnolia

She stopped to smell the Magnolias

So I picked one

Now I walk by everyday

Stopping at that Magnolia tree

Just to smell her

Free as an "Eagle"

Do you dare to be free?
It's a lie we've been sold
We're all but prisoners
Consumed by consumerism
Slaves to the elite
To our thoughts
To the state
To society
To culture
To others perception
As well as to our own
We are birds in a cage
Sitting in *safety*
From the Vultures of Capitalism
Desperate to fly
But crippled by fear
And bound by its limits
But should you begin to molt
And shed the skin you've molded
If the cage door opens
Would you fly?
Would you soar?
Would you dare to be free?
Be you?
Simply be?

Summer Rain

There's just something so soothing

About the patter of rain

On a warm Summers day

The Magician

He walked by me
And from beneath his sleeve
I caught a glimpse of the art
Inked into his arm
Though just half in view
I recognized that tarot card
The Magician
And on the bottom it read
Go Forward Into Your craft
That's all I remember from that dream
...I guess that's a sign

My Apothecary

She sends sweet serotonin
Swimming through my bloodstream
Daffodil daydreams drip dopamine
Tapping my veins
Relaxing my brain
Mending my muscles and mind
With Chamomile smiles
Lush lashes on batted eyes
Sends me spiraling and crashing like thunder
Scents captured in the tresses of her hair
Lulls of Lavender
Soothe me into slumber
Laying waste to my nightmares
And ridding me of despair
The botanical musings
Of this tea leaf reader
With the herbal remedy
Of my choosing
She's a Natural magical healer
No snake oil dealer
I drink her waters
The ancient elixirs
An aid to all ailments
Honeysuckle nectars of nourishment
Drip Like honey on a spoon
The tonic trickles down my tongue
Healing my entire body of its wounds

Becoming whole, as we become one

Potentilla

It was a pleasant surprise
Angel wings running down the back
Pristine feathers in violet black
Such a curious sight
When the tips met hips
A violet flame burned bright
That one forgotten night
In all those sessions
It was then that I understood
Those therapeutic lessons

Hibiscus

The hibiscus vines
Grow down the spine
And make roots
In the fertile ground
Soft gaze – soft sounds
Nascent – transient
Delicate – quiet
Radiant with a tropical warmth
Impossible to pass its charm
Living in the moment
Short lived – potent

Vanilla

Silky smooth
Milky white
Creamy soft
Porcelain shine
It may be Plane Jane to you
But that scent
And flavor
...Lingers
& course through me
Like the warmth of nostalgia
Every season
All year
Always
Say what you will,
There is nothing Vanilla about Vanilla

An Anchor vs The Anchor

It could be a God complex

Some sort of self-righteousness

Or perhaps a sliver of narcissism,

But I've always thought myself an anchor.

Grounding those with safety in stormy seas

But the metaphor was lost on me...

It seems

I'm the anchor that sinks the swimmer

The dead weight dragging you down

When you're ready to take flight

The accidental arsonist

Who sets a heart ablaze,

But burns everything to the ground along with it

I am the anchor holding you down

Holding you back

Weeping Willow

As children
We hung from the arms
Of this graceful giant
Swinging from the branches
And climbing her limbs
Our favorite place to be
Hiding within the curtains
Of her wispy sweeping leaves
Her strength
Only increased as she aged
Her whimsical words of wisdom
Playful as it was sage
The deep crevices in her bark
Like the wrinkles in time
And even in her dying breath
She laughed and smiled

Twin Flower

Rivals and friends from the beginning
Since conception,
A shared home in separate rooms
Just one minute
But everything is a competition
On different sides of the womb
Two ends of the spectrum
Different sides of everything
Never really connected
Nevertheless,
We find connection
In the many characters
Who share this connection
Though not as close
Still I toast
To our Brothers Bond

Darkness

Darkness

On the dark side of midnight
The mind plays tricks
On the eyes and ears
Creaking floorboards
and expanding pipes moans
Create the haunting sounds
of murderous drones
Silhouettes in the shadows
Of coats and piles of clothes
Become monsters under moonlight
Ghosts on my back
Demons in my mind
The Damn Phantoms
Keep me up all night!

Hello*

Hello Heartache, My old friend

Hello Pain, we meet again

Hello Whiskey, my go to amends

Hello Life, I need an end

Hello Lord, your forgiving hand

...Can I start again?

Hello

Hello - Heartache, my old friend
Hello Pain, we meet again
Hello Whiskey, my go to amend
Hello Life, I need an end
Hello lord, with your forgiving hand
... Can I start again?

Seeds of Doubt

Seeds sown into the soil of my soul
Growing from beneath the soles
And into my heart
Spreading roots
Stretching out like branches
Wrapped around bone
Up into the chambers of my skull
And through the labyrinth of my mind
Like a model—
Maudlin
Gazing at his own eyes
Peering into the reflected soul
Through the looking glass
Longing for certainty
In the windows of vanity
Insecurity growing en masse
In this dark mirror
There is little sand left in this hourglass
And little time left on Earth
Before I decay in the dirt,
Do I leap fearlessly forward
or question my every word?
Living life–
Like *A Dream Deferred*

Midnight Blooms

In the hush of the evening
She opens
Fragrant and fearless
Her tenderness waits for darkness
The dawn teaches her to fold herself shut
Daylight asks to be armored and composed
But Night gives permission to soften
To confess –
To be seen for a few quiet hours
Opening only when the world is silent enough to
listen
Nocturnal in her truth
The rush of the day has never been gentle
To opened petals
So, she's learned when it's safe to bloom
In the breaking sun
Tucking vulnerability back into the shadows
Where the world cannot bruise
But as it slips into that sedated slumber
She awakens to life
High on midnight
Queen of the night!

The Dead Bride's Groom

Laid to rest
In her wedding dress
Forever a Bride
Locked in a tomb
In the City of the Dead
He couldn't say goodbye
To the decomposed future
Now just dust for the Past

Spells were cast
For love to last

The fading flesh
Renewed & fresh
On the Dark Side of Midnight
There she stood
In her tattered dress
Once again
They'd stand
Hand in hand
A forever necromance

Every month
Out from her tomb
They'd have their *First Dance*
Under a spotlight moon

Static *

I'm so Static

Head full of white noise

Radio static

Dead Air silence in the void

I'm so static

Dragging my feet in reverse

I feel the static

Pins and needles in my bones

I'm so static

Stasis of my blood turning cold

I'm so static

Static

Static!

A Single Rose

I remember it clearly
It hung in the kitchen
A single rose
Upon the wooden frame
The words *I love you*
Surrounding its lay
Behind it perched a picture
Of me
In my boyhood days

And on the coffee mug
She drank tea from every day
A single rose
Centered beneath
Was her name
In time it would all fade
But still, she drank from only that mug
And still to this day!

And in the kitchen
Still hangs that frame

Alone on the World Stage

Loneliness
They say,
Begs company
But I find,
Loneliness begets solitude
The quiet safe space to feel misery
Without the judgment of prying eyes
Void of inspirational words from naive tongues
Without the expectation to smile
At the lack luster of life
Just for a sip of serotonin
This beast of burden
Carrying the load of others
Dismantling my knees
Hunching my back and shoulders
Burying my own feelings
For fear of suffocating others

At times I crumble
Knees break
& the tummy tumbles
So tired of the fight
Eager for flight
To run away
Into the arms of misery
Finding solace in the silence of solitude
Returning to the dark corners of my mind

And just feel pain
Instead, I am constantly showing up
With a suppressor, silencing the shots
That are firing through my brain
Numbing the wounds riddled throughout my body
Like some walking opiate
A masochist masquerading as a man of comedy
With a belly boiling beneath bottles of tragedy

...And thus, a revelation to feeling nothing
I don't allow myself to feel the pain
To let the blood spill
If I can't feel the pain of being alive
How can I feel the elation of it?

And so,
Loneliness
Allows me to be alone
With myself and the weight that's almost too much
to bear
Allowing it to crush me for a moment
Reminding me I can breathe
And it's then that I realize
I want to experience the density and vibrancy of this
world
I want to feel it all

Shadow Boxer

I set my stance
But like my reflection
He's a southpaw
I prepare
With clasped hands
And clenched fists
Swinging at air
Fighting myself
Punching down the darkness
Muscle memory
Trained to tame
The tragic traits of me
But I created it
In my eclipse
What if I didn't fight?
Didn't repel
My most disgusting self
Seeds of doubt
Plume the dark within
It's time I lay down my arms
Accept the scars of harm

But how?
This monster
This beast-like Hyde
This contaminant

I must look upon with new sight
For He is me and I Am him
He is no demon to exorcise

He is...
The lost boy
The battle-hardened soldier
The beast of burden
The *in pain*

I've heard them say
"Get out of your own way!"

After all...
What is a shadow
If not you impeding the light?

Soldier Boy

On the shores of New York

From the West Indies

Circa 1983

And into the Army

Cold Steel Infantry

Back to the Kissing Bridge

Seawall of Georgetown

And his runaway bride to be

Off to the Springs of Fort Carson

From the Boroughs of the city

Living life

As young couples should be

Off to Germany

And a Wife carrying

The Wall Fell

To a reborn Germany

Born alongside

Were two boys, twin babies

Deployed to the Gulf

Into the battlefield

M16 in arms

Leaving behind his family

Next Station to Germany

Deployed to Bosnia

Into the battlefield

Letters in the mail

I still have the stationery

The day the soldiers returned
I remember it vividly
Running between uniforms
Yelling Frightfully
Terrified he wouldn't return
But he embraced me
And I was elated
Free of that anxiety
We swam in his BDUs
My Brother and Me
Obsessing over camouflage
And everything military
The towers fell
Retirement came, luckily
Though those boots saw no blood
They marched to the service of
The Red handed, White collared, Blue-blooded thugs
Finding our forever-civilian-home circa 2003
On the edge of youth, towards manhood
He told us sternly
"I've served enough years for you both"
So we stayed Army Brats proudly

Desert Rose

How beautiful
Such a poisonous creature

The Violet Affair

Stealing glances
Disguising touches
Walking by
Brushing hands
That velvet voice
Whispers with lush
Lullabies in the ear
The tremor of being near
Orchestrated meet cutes
And secret rendezvous
Only by night
Silent love fills the air
In the neon lights
Of A Violet Affair

Whiskey & Cigarettes

Sweet memories
Put bitters on my tongue
Breathing daydreams
Like smoke in my lungs

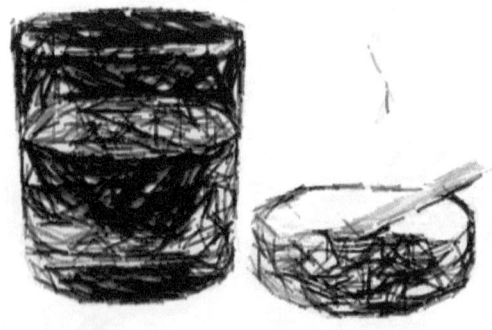

Wolfsbane

Under the light of the moon

I howl

The echo returns

Empty

Mythical Weapons loom

In the hunt she leads

With her toxic touch

The wolfsbane burns

But I can't get enough

I break my bones

To transform

Becoming something feared and powerful

Under the light of the moon

I turn

And her hunt begins

To tame this beast

She puts this Wolf down

So easily

Kiss of the Vampire

They call me a monster
But I'm far from savage

For thousands of years
This undead soul has walked this Earth
And only now I've come alive

In a collection of countless encounters
Lost to the long march of time
It's your skin I sink my teeth in

For the first time my fangs feed
For pleasure not sustenance

Your blood, immortalized in me
Centuries of endless eyes entranced under my spell
But your hypnotic hips have me compelled

With the salivating drips
Of bloodlust on my lips

Thousands of years I've waited
Millennia, Longing with desire

Captured on my tongue, now evaded
Nothing seems to curb these cravings

But should the stars be in my favor

Should I once again sample your flavor

I will attempt to slow time and make you last

For your taste, I will forever savor

R.I.P J.J. Paulson

Would anyone even miss me?
I realized, today,
If tragedy were to befall me
Not one person could conjure
A comment to compliment
Would I be such a loss
Or perhaps
Sweet relief of a burden no longer to bear?
I think the latter
As I look upon my life
And my ripple effect across time
I oscillate ... only pain.
What blissful freedom would it be
In a world without me?

...except maybe for Princess

Big Lawn

The Lawn – is a border wall of grass
A sermon preached in green
Green – spread ideology
A gospel of control
Stretching suburb to suburb
Like a campaign ad for order

Each blade must stand to attention
Each edge sharpened like an invoice
Trimmed to acceptable height
The way workers are trimmed
To acceptable lives
Uniform. Replaceable.
Obedient to the mower's logic

Behind it's manicured calm
The soil beneath hums
With endless unpaid overtime—
A pulse of endless labor:
Grow, but not too much;
Live, but only this way;
Be green, be neat, be identical
Be what we need you to be
For our pockets of green
The lawn's own military budget
Defending its smooth green nation – state
It demands tribute—

Water, fuel, chemicals
The buzz of machines
That keep its uniform face smiling for the neighbors

And there, in the cracks
The quiet scratching of weeds rise
Dreaming their unruly dreams
Dandelions waving yellow fists
Clover forming underground unions
Wild plantain broadcasting the good news
That freedom often looks like disorder

But the lawn tells a different story—
A propaganda campaign against anything
That grows without buying something first
"Weeds are bad" big lawn instructs,
Things that thrive outside the market
Must be criminalized
Diversity that can't be monetized
Must be sprayed out of existence

Yet still the weeds return
Like grassroots movements do
Quiet revolutions
Whispering alternative futures
Through the cracks of capitalism's
Carefully manicured veneer

Mushrooms Leave Their Marx

In the Dim humus of the forest
Threads travel like whispered promises
Mycelium, pale as moon breath
Weaves a network from root to root
In this rainbow coalition
A quiet covenant:
"No one here stands alone"

Beneath the soil
No hierarchy—
Only communion
A democracy of decay and renewal
Every death an offering
Every life a shared inheritance

Beneath the forest's voting booth of roots
Mycelium drafts its own constitution –
A sprawling, translucent bill of rights
Where nourishment is a shared clause
And scarcity is a myth whispered
By those who never learned how forests feed

Food passes
From the fed to the hungry
From the strong to the wilted
Like a secret generosity
Older than kings of days past

Or ancient clocks
Here, the radicals are soft bodied
And quiet as a dawn fog
Yet they organize better than any parliament
A thousand tiny connections
Redistributing carbon
Faster than a senator can clear his throat

Mushrooms rise – humble emissaries
From the worker soil
Of a world where wealth
Is the forest's
Not the fortunate's
Their caps small red manifestos
Against the myth of the solitary tree

No hero trees here
No bootstraps
No moralizing about who deserves sunlight
In this republic of rot and resurgence
Every fallen leaf is welfare
Every corpse is a community investment
And all futures are grown cooperatively
In solidarity

Planted Earth

So many a majestic miles

Measures this medley meadow

A denizens of color

Red

White

Violets

And Yellows

Such a variety

How easy to be unheard and unseen

To feel overshadowed and lost

In the constant calamity

And chaos

Each one a story of their own

Deserving a chance to grow

To photosynthesize

And come alive

And rightfully so!

You may not be the center of the Universe

But you are the center of Yours

Proof

Of all the flowers to bloom

In a world of beauty and gloom

This is my proof –

That I picked you

Even then

And when I atomize

Becoming once again stardust

Vaporized

Out of sight to the naked eye

Particles scattered

Into the void with the dark matter

You'll still be a part of me

Sent hurdling together

across the vast endless space

And when I realign

Once again carbonized

There you will be

Still a part of me

Still alive

A Long Passage on My Opinion of Love

Love is a Force
A Cosmic Certainty
Not a feeling, but it is felt
The weight of it like gravity
A push and pull like magnets
Bringing particles into collision
Sending souls spiraling
Falling into each others orbit
Eternally entangled
Infinitely intertwined
The ailment of alignment
It transcends space and time
It is beyond life and death
But how often the word so easily spills
Off our twisting tongues
Polluting its meaning
And diluting its power
It is not blind, but clear in sight
It is not chemical
Nor is it a passionate romance
Even Self-love often inflates into vanity
Human hubris
Confusing and dissolving its essence with
Obsession
Longing
Worship
Lust

All anecdotal attempts to define it
Wasted in youthful haste

But the beauty of Love is

It is beyond our understanding
Kindness, compassion, free of envy,
Forgiveness, unselfish unconditional benevolence
Are mere compositions of its symphony
But no polite summation does it justice
It is boundless, limitless, and endless
Never wrong
In our ignorance we adhere it to rules, terms and
conditions
Create it a law
But it is The law

It just IS
And it is Just

In its purity, beyond our comprehension
A sense, beyond senses
An unknown until it is known
By cells constantly consumed by it
Jettison us into new dimensions
And nothing is left
But the omnipresence of us
Woven within
The tapestry of the universe

A perfect harmony
The force that holds it all together

To the wars raging within hearts
To all our external conflicts
To all our problems, woes, and sorrows
In a world full of suffering, malice and hate
To all our questions

Our reason for being...

... The Answer ...

Is

Love

.

* – These poems were originally songs. Either parts of a song, a line from a song, or the idea/concept for a song.

Thank You